MONKEYS
THE JAPANESE MACAQUES

by Cynthia Overbeck

Photographs by Osamu Nishikawa

A Lerner Natural Science Book

Lerner Publications Company ▪ Minneapolis

Sylvia A. Johnson, Series Editor

Translation by Kay Kushino
Additional research by Jane Dallinger

LIBRARY OF CONGRESS CATALOGING IN PUBLICATION DATA

Overbeck, Cynthia.
    Monkeys: the Japanese macaques.

    (A Lerner natural science book)
    Adapted from Japanese monkeys by O. Nishikawa,
originally published under title: Nihonzaru.
    Includes index.
    Summary: Describes the macaque monkeys of Japan
and explains how they have learned to survive the
cold, snowy winters on the northern island of Honshu.
    1. Japanese macaque—Juvenile literature. [1. Japanese
macaque. 2. Monkeys] I. Nishikawa, Osamu, 1940-
II. Nishikawa, Osamu, 1940-   Nihonzaru. III. Title.
IV. Series: Lerner natural science book.

QL737.P93093   599.8'2   81-1961
    ISBN 0-8225-1464-8   AACR2

This edition first published 1981 by Lerner Publications Company.
Revised text copyright © 1981 by Lerner Publications Company.
Photographs copyright © 1971 by Osamu Nishikawa.
Adapted from JAPANESE MONKEYS copyright © 1971 by
Osamu Nishikawa. English language rights arranged by
Japan UNI Agency, Inc. for Akane Shobo Publishers, Tokyo.

International Standard Book Number: 0-8225-1464-8
Library of Congress Catalog Card Number: 81-1961

1 2 3 4 5 6 7 8 9 10 90 89 88 87 86 85 84 83 82 81

A Note on Scientific Classification

The animals in this book are sometimes called by their scientific names as well as by their common English names. These scientific names are part of the system of **classification**, which is used by scientists all over the world. Classification is a method of showing how different animals (and plants) are related to each other. Animals that are alike are grouped together and given the same scientific name.

Those animals that are very much like one another belong to the same **species** (SPEE-sheez). This is the basic group in the system of classification. An animal's species name is made up of two words in Latin or Greek. For example, the species name of the lion is *Panthera leo*. This scientific name is the same in all parts of the world, even though an animal may have many different common names.

The next smallest group in scientific classification is the **genus** (GEE-nus). A genus is made up of more than one species. Animals that belong to the same genus are closely related but are not as much alike as the members of the same species. The lion belongs to the genus *Panthera*, along with its close relatives the leopard, *Panthera pardus*, the tiger, *Panthera tigris*, and the jaguar, *Panthera onca*. As you can see, the first part of the species name identifies the animal's genus.

Just as a genus is made up of several species, a **family** is made up of more than one genus. Animals that belong to the same family are generally similar but have some important differences. Lions, leopards, tigers, and jaguars all belong to the family Felidae, a group that also includes cheetahs and domestic cats.

Families of animals are parts of even larger groups in the system of classification. This system is a useful tool both for scientists and for people who want to learn about the world of nature.

People have always enjoyed watching monkeys in zoos. These lively animals never seem to get tired of climbing and swinging in their cages. But how much better it is to see monkeys living in the wild. Scientists who have studied monkeys in their natural surroundings have learned many fascinating things about their habits and behavior. One kind of monkey that has been frequently studied is the macaque (muh-KAK).

Some Japanese macaques make their homes in cold, mountainous areas (*left*), while others live on sunny beaches (*right*).

There are about 50 species of macaques in the world. Most of them live in Asia and the islands of the Pacific, but one kind of macaque is found in North Africa. A small group of macaques also lives in the tiny area called Gibraltar, located on the southern coast of Spain. The macaques in this book are natives of Japan. They are members of the species *Macaca fuscata*.

Japanese macaques live in many different kinds of conditions and climates. In Japan, a country made up of four main islands, the climate varies widely. The southern islands of Kyushu and Shikoku have moderate weather. Here, the macaques live along the beaches and in the forests. On Honshu, the largest island, the climate ranges from moderate to extreme. At the island's center are steep mountains called the Japanese Alps. There, winters are long and cold, with driving snow and freezing temperatures. Yet groups of hardy macaques have found ways to live even in this harsh climate.

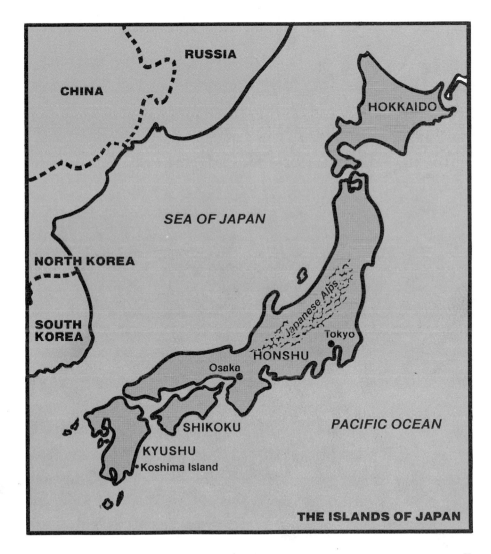

THE ISLANDS OF JAPAN

Right: A baby macaque nursing. Like other monkeys, macaques are mammals, animals whose babies live on milk from their mothers' bodies.

The lives of most Japanese macaques begin in the spring or summer. When a baby macaque is born, it has all the special body features that it will need to survive. But at the beginning, the baby is tiny and undeveloped. A newborn macaque is only about 4 inches (10 centimeters) long and weighs less than a pound (.45 kilograms). Its large eyes open soon after birth, but they cannot focus on objects.

The only parts of the infant macaque's body that are well developed at birth are its tiny hands. Soon after it is born, the baby can cling tightly to its mother's fur. It is able to do this because its little hands have an important feature that is shared by most other monkeys. The hands have what scientists call **opposable thumbs**. This means that the thumb moves independently of the other fingers. Opposable thumbs allow macaques to grasp tree branches firmly as they climb and to pick up and hold objects. Macaques can also use their feet to grasp because, like the thumbs, the big toes move independently.

The baby macaque must hold on tightly to its mother's fur in order to survive. Japanese macaques move from place to place during the day in search of food, and the mother must keep up with the group. As the mother moves along, the baby rides under her belly, hanging on tightly to her fur.

Left: Like most monkeys, Japanese macaques can pick up and hold small objects with their hands or feet.

Right: A baby macaque rides under its mother's belly as she moves along on all four legs.

Although a macaque is helpless when it is first born, it grows quickly. When the baby is about a week old, it begins to crawl around on the ground near its mother. It also tries climbing, pulling itself up on its mother's fur with its hands.

It is not long before the baby's eyes are strong and can focus. A macaque's eyes are another important tool for survival. Their most useful feature is their ability to judge distance. It is this ability that makes it possible for the monkeys to move safely from branch to branch high in the treetops. Living in the trees helps to keep macaques safe from dangerous animals on the ground. The monkeys also depend on their eyesight, as well as their good hearing, to warn them of danger.

While a macaque is still a baby, however, it depends completely on its mother to protect and take care of it. The little macaque must be taught how to survive. The mother helps her baby to learn what foods to eat. She also encourages the baby to walk, climb, and learn other necessary skills.

13

A baby macaque plays on the ground near its mother.

As the baby macaque grows, it continues to stay close to
its mother. Her nearness helps the baby to feel safe. The
little monkey also enjoys keeping in close contact with its
mother's warm body.

15

Left: One young macaque grooms another.

Right: A mother cleans her baby's hands and face.

Touching is very important to macaques and to other monkeys. Adult macaques spend a lot of time hugging and holding their babies. Most macaques, both adults and youngsters, also keep in touch with one another through the action called **grooming**. A mother begins grooming her baby soon after it is born. She uses her hands to pick through the baby's fur, pulling out dirt and bugs that have gotten caught there.

As the baby grows up, it will learn to groom and be groomed by other macaques. Grooming is an important social activity for the macaques as well as a way of keeping clean. The monkeys seem to love the feeling of being groomed, and they relax completely while it takes place.

By the time a baby macaque is about three weeks old, it has learned to walk. Like most macaques, the baby walks on all four legs. It moves in a kind of gallop or frog leap. As it grows, the baby learns new skills rapidly. At three or four months, it is strong enough to climb up on its mother's back and hang on. Now it can ride along on top instead of clinging to the mother's belly.

18

At this time the baby also begins to eat solid food in addition to drinking its mother's milk. Like most monkeys, macaques eat leaves, bark, fruit, grains, vegetables, and insects. Babies must be taught by their mothers which foods to eat. But sometimes young macaques experiment with new foods. If these foods prove to be acceptable, a whole group of macaques may begin to eat them. The way in which macaques learn new eating habits shows their intelligence and learning ability.

A baby macaque learning to pick up wheat grains by copying its mother

In order to find out more about how macaques learn, Japanese scientists have been studying a group of macaques on Koshima Island, off the coast of Kyushu. When the study began in 1953, the monkeys lived in the thick forest in the center of the island. But the scientists used food to get the macaques to come out onto the island's beaches. Now the Koshima macaques spend most of their time on the beach, where the scientists can watch their behavior.

One of the foods that the scientists gave the macaques was wheat, which they scattered on the sandy beach. At first the macaques had trouble separating the grains of wheat from the sand. But they soon solved the problem. They saw that when they threw a handful of sand and wheat into the water, the heavier sand sank, and the wheat grains floated. That made it easy to pick up the wheat. The macaques often pick up a lot of wheat at one time and store it in small pouches in their cheeks to eat later on.

These macaques have learned to walk on their hind legs so that they can use their hands to carry things.

Another food that macaques on Koshima have learned to eat is the sweet potato. One young female discovered that she liked the salty taste her potatoes had after she washed them in the ocean water. She began washing all her potatoes. Eventually all the macaques in her group copied her.

Washing the potatoes also led to a change in the macaques' behavior. Normally, macaques walk on all fours, using both hands and feet. But now they needed their hands to carry the sweet potatoes to the water. So the macaques learned to walk upright on their hind legs. This left their hands free to carry food. Now, this group of Koshima macaques has a special new skill.

Such discoveries are usually made by the younger macaques. Other youngsters are the first to copy them. Eventually the older macaques learn, too. Finally the mothers pass on the new habit or skill to their babies along with the old habits.

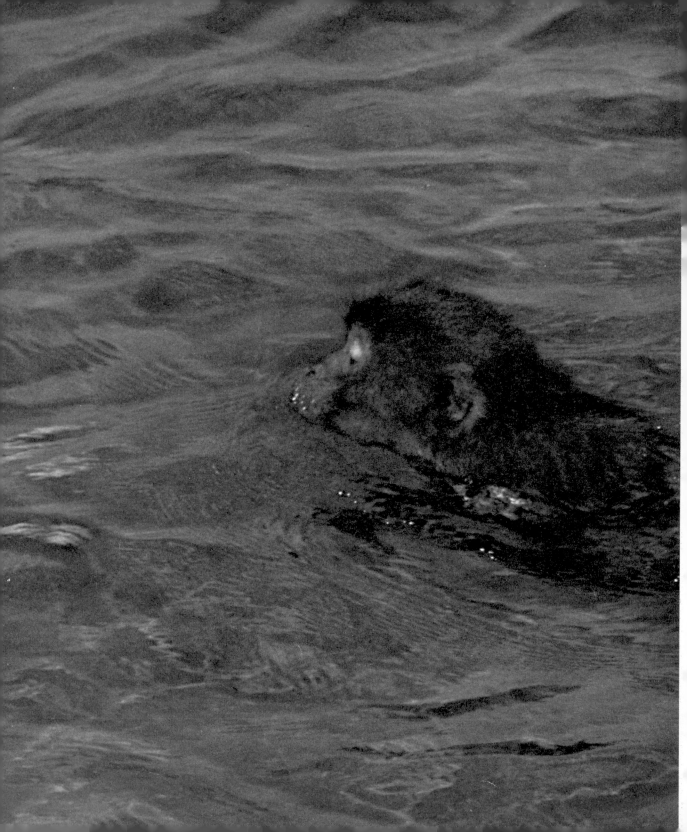

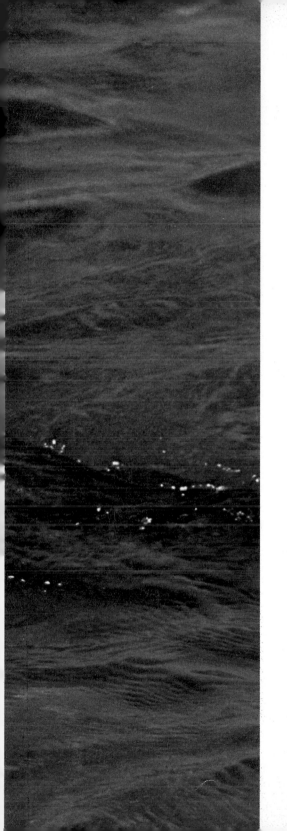

Yet another change in behavior came about among the Koshima macaques because of their experience with new foods. When scientists threw food out into the water instead of on the beach, the macaques began swimming out to get it. Soon, the young macaques invented new water games to play. As time went on, they spent more and more time in the water.

All these examples show the amazing ability of some macaques to learn new habits. Often, these new ways of behaving help them to improve the way in which they live in their environment.

25

As young macaques grow larger and stronger and learn new skills, their relationship with their mothers changes. Macaques up to a year old or more may still want their mother's milk (above). But by the age of about three to five months, most youngsters no longer feel the need to stay close to their mothers all the time.

Instead, they begin to take an interest in the world around them. They are lively, curious creatures, and they love to explore. On the beaches they tumble and run over the sand. In the forests they learn to be at home in the treetops, climbing up to high branches and playing there with ease.

Left: Macaques are as much at home in the trees as they are on the ground.

Young macaques spend a lot of time playing with each other. Playing among themselves is one way in which the youngsters copy adult behavior and learn the ways of the group.

Japanese macaques live in groups called **troops**, which are made up of 30 or more members. Group life is very important to the macaques. It is group cooperation that helps them to find food and to protect themselves from danger.

A macaque troop has a strict social order and strict rules of behavior. It is led by one adult male who has authority over all the rest of the members. This leader is usually one of the strongest males. He often wins his position in a fight with other males or with the previous troop leader.

Every other member of the troop—male, female, and youngster—has its own position in the troop. Some of the monkeys are recognized as superior to the others because of their strength or perhaps their intelligence. Scientists call these monkeys the **dominant** (DAHM-eh-nunt) members of the troop. The dominant macaques take the first place in the activities of the troop. At meal times, for example, they get the best food and the privilege of eating first.

Two young macaques play together on the beach.

From the troop leader down to the weakest member, each macaque knows its place in the group. Young macaques quickly learn their proper positions. In their games, the strong youngsters and the weak ones work out their relationships with one another. They chase each other and have wrestling matches to see who is the strongest.

Young macaques often have the same kind of position in the troop that their mothers have. Babies of dominant mothers, for example, will usually grow up to be dominant themselves. The members of dominant families have strong ties with each other. Relationships are close among mothers, sisters, brothers, aunts, and cousins. Brothers and sisters often stay near each other, playing and eating together long after they have grown up.

In these pictures, a group of brothers has formed a small "gang" to tease some of the other young macaques in the troop.

A troop leader watches some young macaques at play.

But no matter how much they tease one another, all the macaques, young and old, must respect the troop leader. The whole troop depends on him, and he is responsible for their safety. The macaques are often in danger from wild dogs, bears, and sometimes people. Even though the macaques spend their nights and some of their daylight hours in the trees, they live on the ground during most of the day. They need strong leadership in emergencies.

The troop leader can be fierce. He has great strength and may weigh up to 40 pounds (18 kilograms). His long **canine** teeth are sharp and make good weapons for defense.

In addition to protecting the troop, the leader is responsible for helping all the members to find food. Under normal conditions, macaque troops move from place to place every day, searching for food. Every day the leader must choose a trail for the troop to follow through the countryside. Each night, he chooses the place in the treetops where the troop will rest for the night.

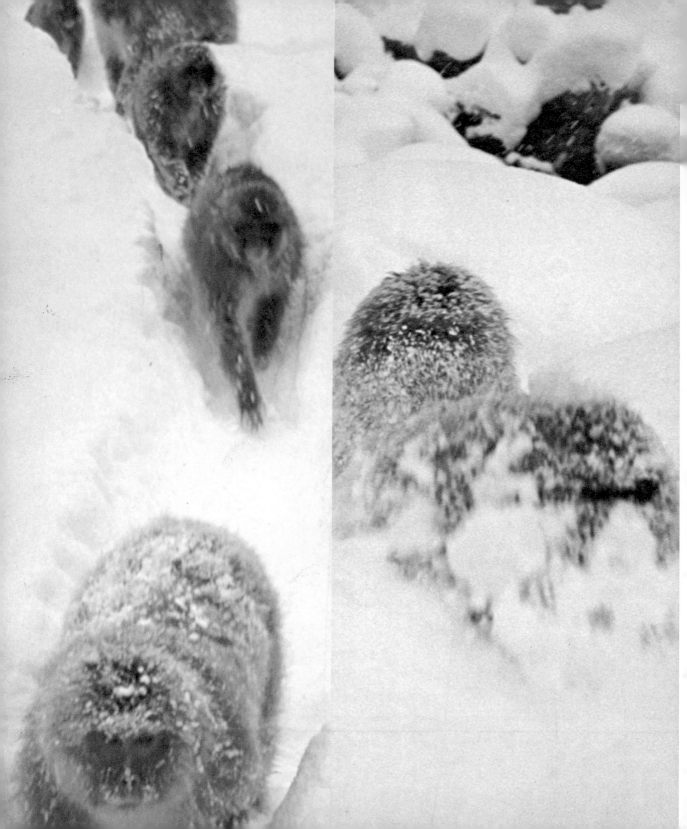

When winter comes to the northern, mountainous parts of Japan, the leader must often clear a path through deep snow for the troop. The macaques that live in these regions have a harder life than those in the southern beaches and forests. These macaques, sometimes called **snow monkeys**, are slightly larger than the southern macaques. They also have longer, shaggier fur to help keep them warm. They need their warm fur, for the snows in midwinter may be over 6 feet (1.8 meters) deep, and temperatures often drop to below freezing.

39

There is little for the macaques to eat in this frozen winter world. They feed mostly on bark, which they strip from tree branches and twigs. The tree branches in areas where macaques have fed often show long, bare scars where the bark has been stripped. The macaques also eat the winter buds of trees and bushes. These are the tightly packed shoots of the new branches that would have grown the next spring.

41

Right and above: Macaques enjoying the warm water of hot springs

In one part of the island of Honshu, the macaques have learned to find temporary relief from the cold by bathing in hot springs. These are pools of water that are heated naturally, winter and summer, through underground channels that carry heat up from deep in the earth. Scientists believe that the macaques go into the water from time to time to warm their bodies during the cold weather.

But when icy winds blow and winter storms rage, the macaques can find few places to hide. They must puff out their fur to trap their own body heat around themselves. The whole troop may huddle together in a group so that all can benefit from the collected body heat. At night, the macaques must cling to the bare treetops in order to stay safe from attacking animals.

Yet in spite of these harsh conditions, the monkeys manage to survive. Like other Japanese macaques, the snow monkeys have learned how to live successfully in their environment.

46

GLOSSARY

canine teeth—long, sharp teeth used for biting and tearing

dominant monkeys—those monkeys that are stronger than and superior to other monkeys in a group

grooming—a form of social activity and mutual cleaning in which one monkey picks through and cleans the fur of another monkey

mammal—a warm-blooded animal that feeds its young with milk from its own body

opposable thumb—a thumb that can move independently of the other fingers on the hand

snow monkey—a name given to those macaques that live in the cold, mountainous regions of Japan

troop—a group of macaques that may include from 30 to 100 males, females, and babies

INDEX